Victorian Design FROM THE Crystal Palace Exhibition

Edited by
Carol Belanger Grafton

Dover Publications, Inc.
Mineola, New York

Copyright

Bibliographical Note

This Dover edition, first published in 2010, contains a new selection of images from the work originally published in 1851 by George Virtue for *The Art-Journal*. A CD-ROM containing all of the images has been included.

DOVER *Pictorial Archive* SERIES

International Standard Book Number
ISBN-13: 078-0-486-47210-5
ISBN-10: 0-486-47219-1

Manufactured in the United States by Courier Corporation
47219101
www.doverpublications.com

NOTE

The Crystal Palace Exhibition of 1851 (also known as the Exhibition of the Industry of All Nations or Great Exhibition) was a showcase for the world to display their accomplishments in modern industrial design and technology. The exhibit took place in Hyde Park, London and was the first in a series of World's Fair exhibitions. Designed by Joseph Paxton, the palace took less than a year to build and housed 14,000 exhibitors within its 990,000 square feet. This collection contains over 640 pieces from the exhibit including chess figures, carved tables, ornamental fountains, and other unique items.

The CD-ROM in this book contains all of the images. Each image has been saved as a 300-dpi high-resolution JPEG and a 72-dpi Internet-ready JPEG. There is no installation necessary. Just insert the CD into your computer and call the images into your favorite software (refer to the documentation with your software for further instructions).

Within the "Images" folder on the CD you will find two additional folders—"High Resolution JPG" and "JPG." Every image has a unique file name in the following format: xxx.JPG. The first 3 characters of the file name correspond to the number printed with the image in the book. The last 3 letters of the file name, JPG, refer to the file format. So, 001.JPG would be the first file in the folder.

Also included on the CD-ROM is Dover Design Manager, a simple graphics editing program for Windows that will allow you to view, print, crop, and rotate the images.

For technical support, contact:
Telephone: 1 (617) 249-0245
Fax: 1 (617) 249-0245
Email: dover@artimaging.com
Internet: http://www.dovertechsupport.com
The fastest way to receive technical support is via email or the Internet.

001

002

003

004

005

006

007

008

1

009

010

011

012

013

015

014

016

017

018

019

020

021

022

023

024

025

026

027

028

029

030

5

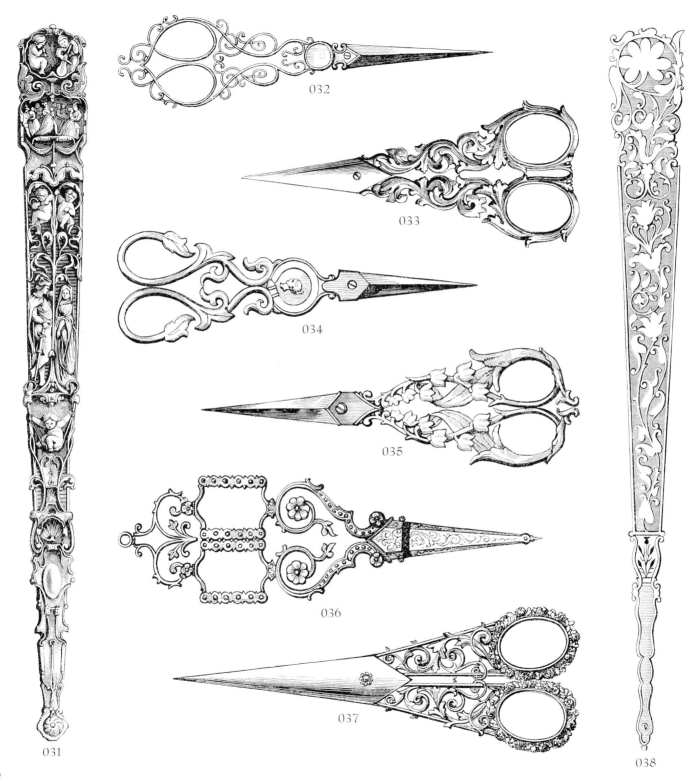

031

032

033

034

035

036

037

038

6

039

041

042

043

044

045

046

047

048

049

050

051

052

9

053

054

055

056

057

058

10

059

060

061

062

11

063

064

065

066

067

068

069

070

071

072

073

074

075

13

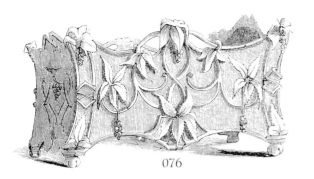

076

077

078

080

079

081

082

083

084

085

086

087

088

089

090

16

091   092   093   094   095

096

097

098

099

100

101

18

102

103

104

105

106

107

19

108

109

110

111

112

113

115

116

117

22 118

119

120

121

122

124

123

125

126

127

128

129

23

130

131

132

133

24 134 135

136

137

138

139

140

141

142

143

144

145

146

147

148

149

150

151

152

153

154

27

155

156

157

158

159

160

161

162

163

164

165

166

167

168

169

170

171

172

173

30

174

175

176

177

178

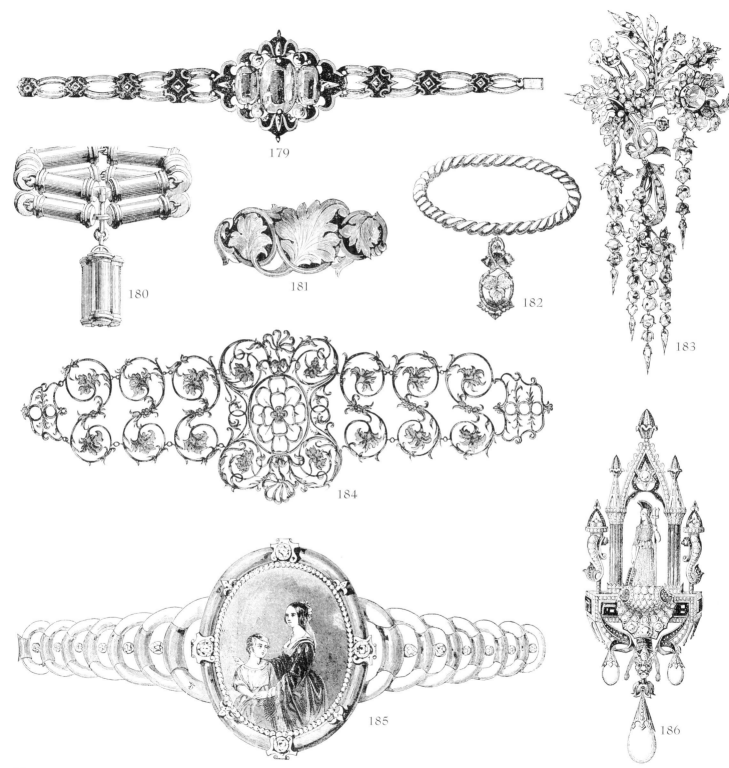

179

180

181

182

183

184

185

186

187

188

189

190

191

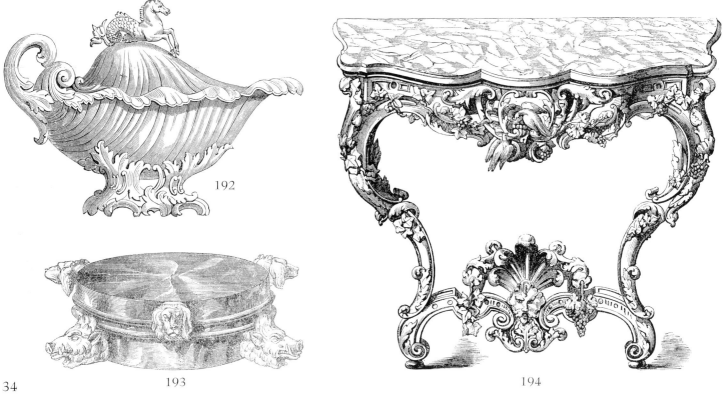

192

193

194

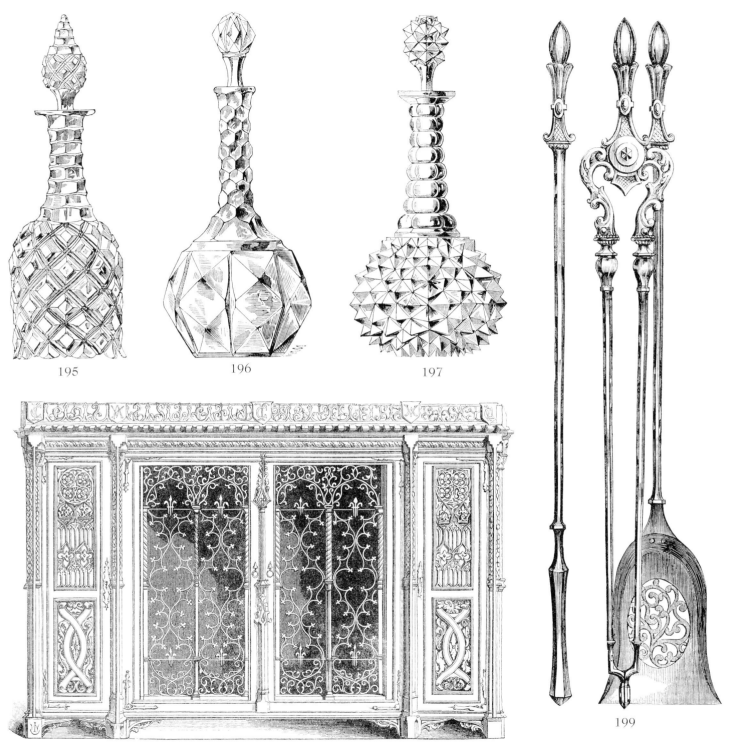

195

196

197

198

199

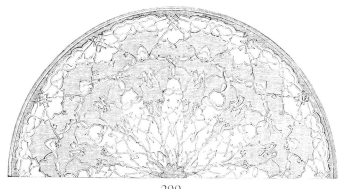

200

201

202

36 203 204

205

206

207

208

209

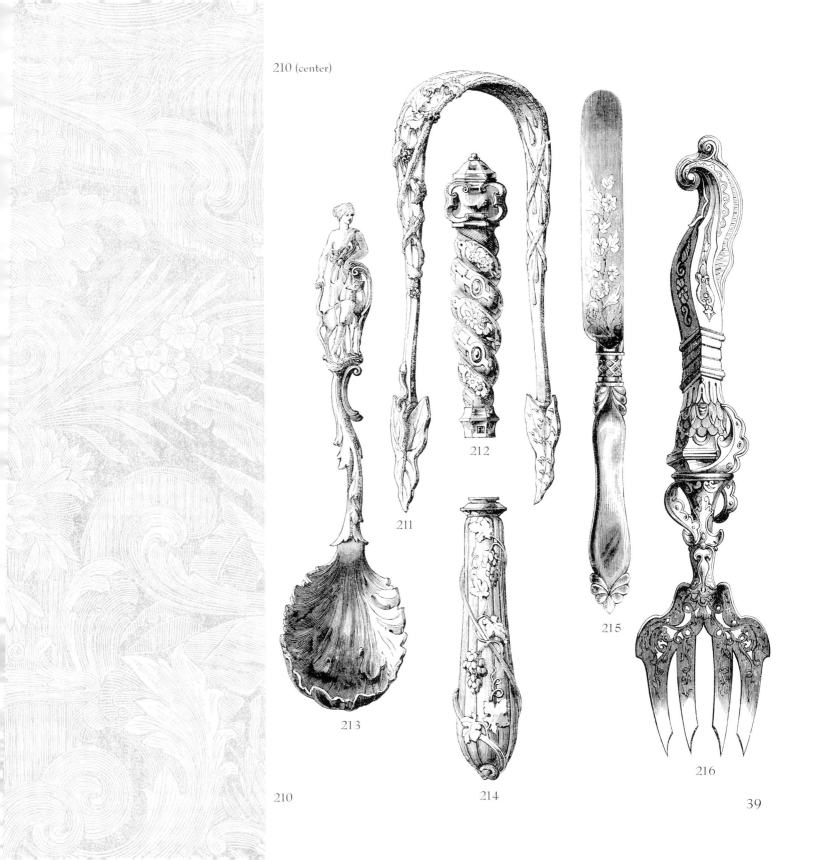

210 (center)

212

211

213

215

214

216

210

39

217

218

219

220

40 221 222

223

224

225

226

227

228

229

230

231

232

233

234

235

236

237

238

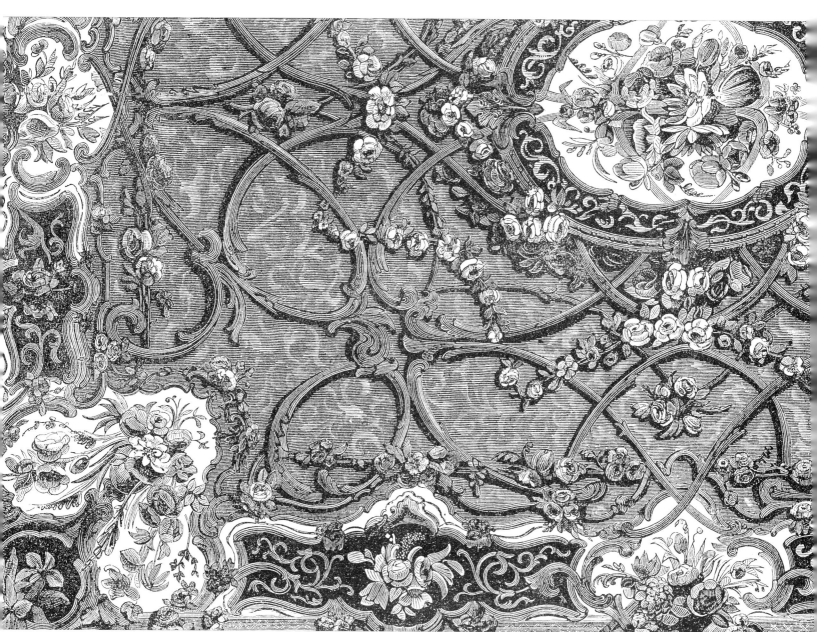

239

240

241

242

243

244

245

246

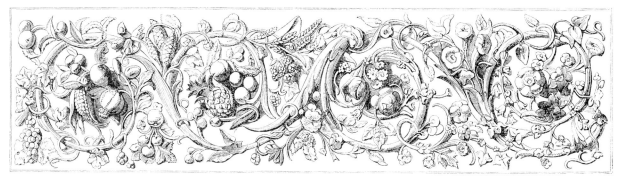

247

248

249

250

251

252

253

254

255

256

257

258

259

260

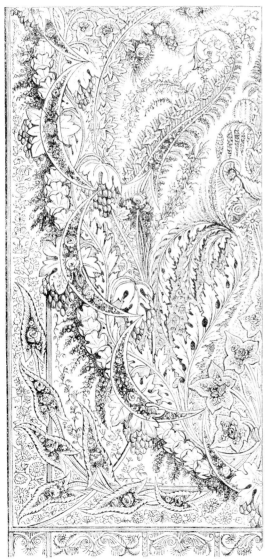

261

263

262

264

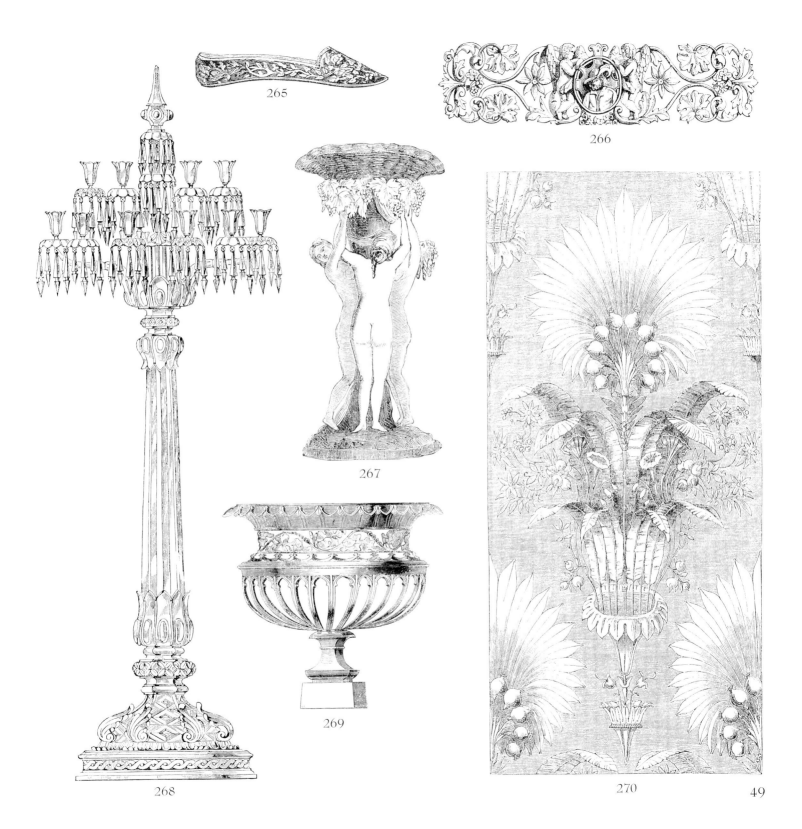

265

266

267

268

269

270

271

272 273 274 275 276 277

278 279 280 281 282 283

284

285

51

287

286

288

289

290

291

292

293

294

295

296

297

298

299

300

301

302

303

304

305

306

307

55

308

309

310

311

312

313

314

315 (center)
315

316

317

318

57

319

320

321

322

323

324

325

326

327

328

59

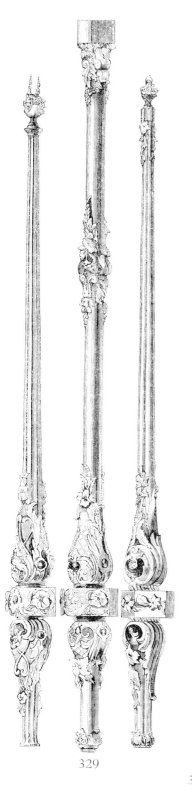

329

330

331

332

333

334   335   336   337

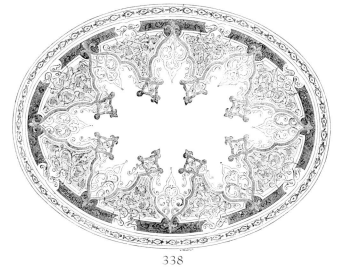

338

339

341

62 340

342

343

344

345

346

347

348

349

64   350   351   352

353

354

355

356

357

358

65

359

360

66   361

362

363

364

365

366

367

368

369

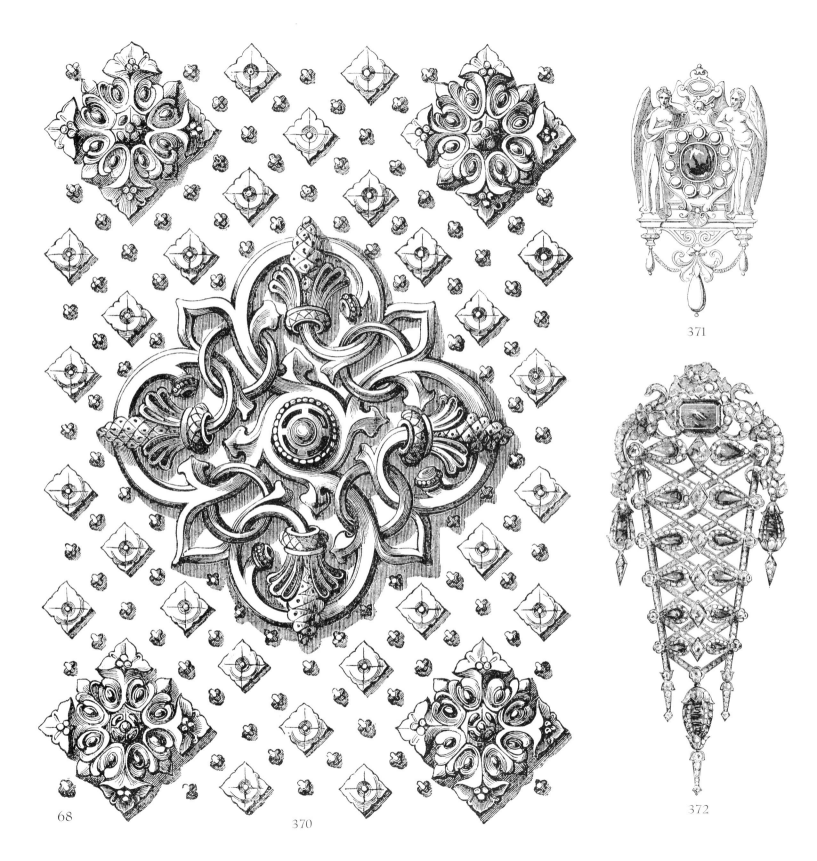

68

370

371

372

373

374

375

376

377

69

379

378

380

381

382

383

384

385

386

387

388

390

389

391

392

393

394

395

396

397

398

399

400

401

402

74   403

404

405

406

407

408

409

410

411

412

413

414

415

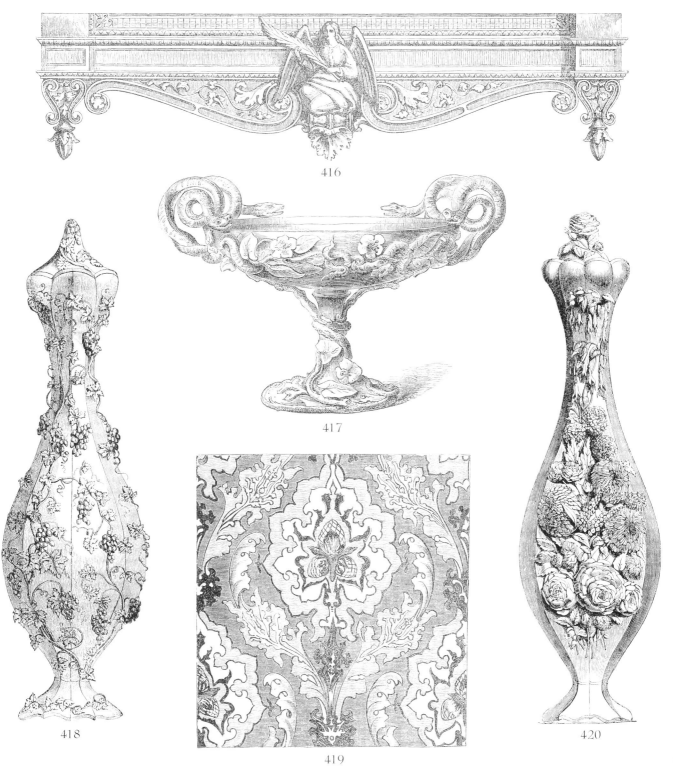

416

417

418

419

420

421

422

423

78 424 425

426

427

428

429

430

431

432

433

434

435

436

437

438

439

440

441

442

443

444

445

446

447

448

449

450

451

452

453

454

455

456

457

458

459

460

461

462

463

464

86 465

466

467

468

469

470

471

472

473

474

475

476

477

478

479

480

481

482

483   484   485

89

486

487

488

489

490

491

492

493

494

91

495

496

497

498

499

92

500

501

502

503

504

505

506

507

94

508

509

510

511

512

513

514

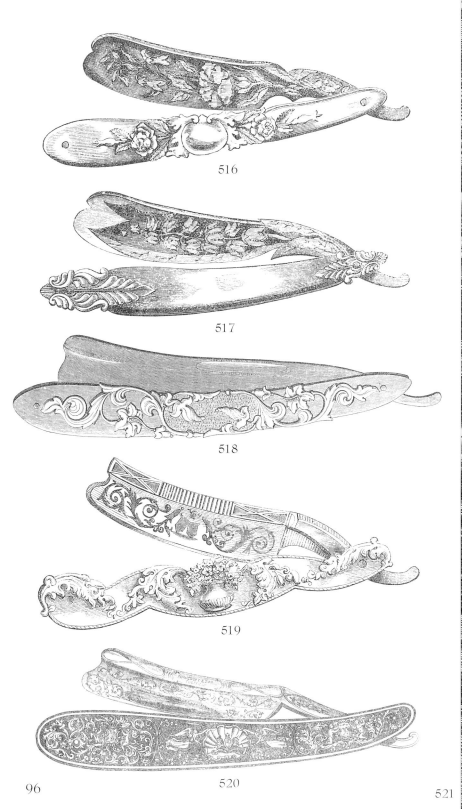

516

517

518

519

520

521

522

523

524

525

526

527

528

529

530

533

534

531

532

535

536

537

538

539

540

100

541

542

543

544

545

546

547

548

549

550

551

552

553

554

555

556

557

104   558   559

560

561

562

563

564

565

566

567

568

569

570

571

572

573

574

575

576

577

578

579

580

581

582

583

584

585

586

587

588

589

590

591

592

593

594

595

596

597

598

599

600

601

602

603

604

605

606

607

608

609

610

611

612

613

114 614

SPIRIT V SNTI AM IN + NOMINE

615

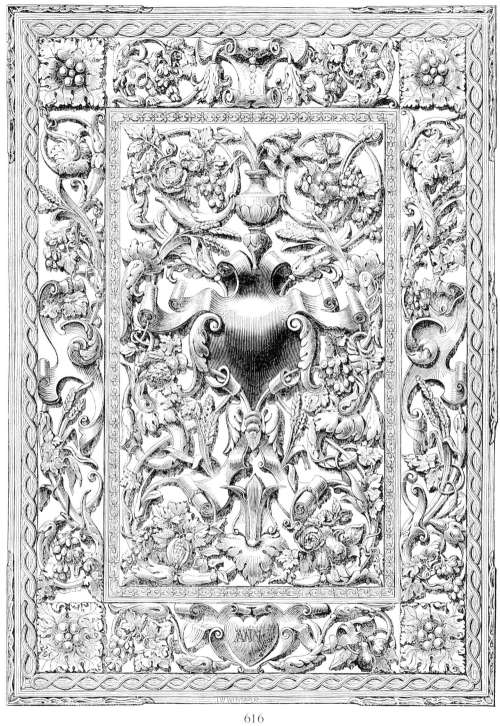

616

617

618

115

619

620

621

622

623

624

625

626

627

628

629

630

631

632

633

118

634

635

636

637

638

639

640

641

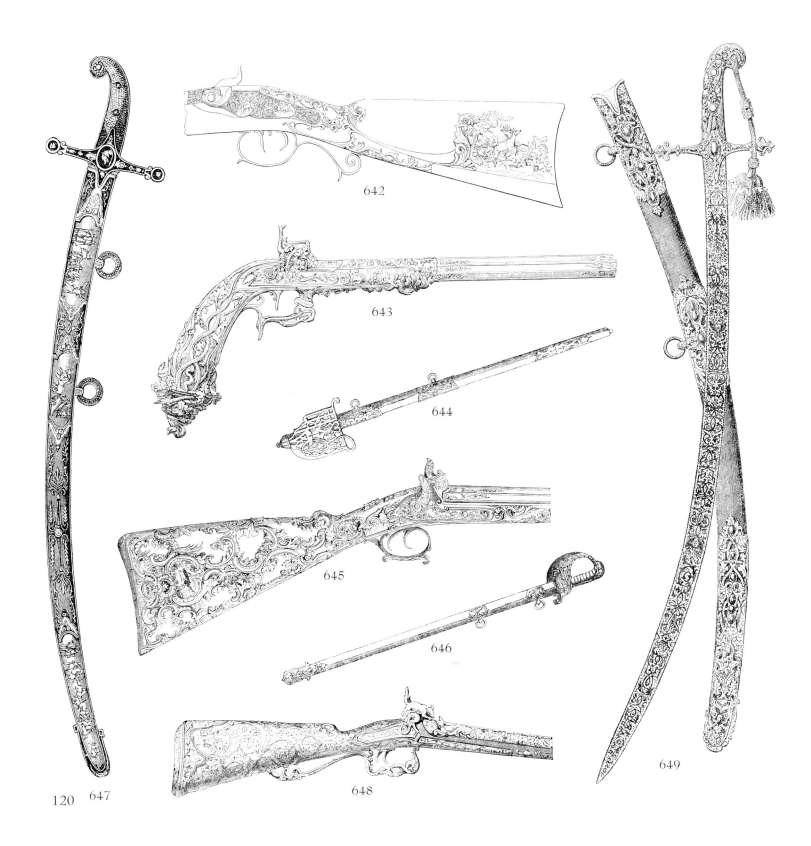

642

643

644

645

646

647

648

649

Guide to the Illustrations

cup and cover of enameled gold and rock crystal. 303. Carved piano. 304. Carved barometer. 305. Chandelier. 306. Table with swans and aquatic plants. 307. Piece from a silver dessert service.

Pages 56–57

308-310, 312-314. Brooches with enamel and jewels. 311. Bracelet with enamel and jewels. 315. Detail from a carpet. 316-318. Brooches.

Pages 58–59

319-322. Enameled watches set with jewels. 323. Italian style bedstead carved in ebony. 324. Watch. 325. Billiard table made of Spanish mahogany. 326. Greek style basin. 327. Terra-cotta pillar. 328. Carved wooden sideboard.

Pages 60–61

329. Bed pillars. 330. Alhambra style damask hanging. 331. Asparagus tongs of magneto-plated silver. 332. Silver-plated dessert fork. 333. Silver-plated cream ladle. 334. Handle of a fish knife. 335. Silver-plated caddy spoon. 336. Spoon for a tea caddy of boxwood. 337. Ivory handle of a bread knife.

Pages 62–63

338. Papier-mâché tray. 339. Chintz furniture pattern. 340. Cabinet of ivory and pear wood. 341. Tazza and cover of chased iron with an enameled center and gold damascene work. 342. Silver gilt casket of the cinquecento period set with gems. 343. Basket of electro-silver plate mounted on carved oak. 344. Cruet frame in an arabesque pattern. 345. Detail from an oak sideboard. 346. Detail from a velvet pile carpet. 347. Bronze ornamental goblet.

Pages 64–65

348, 349. Ornamental vases. 350. Garden vase with serpent handles. 351. Enameled vase with jewels. 352, 358. Silver cups. 353. Silver vase. 354. Papier-mâché tray. 355. Crystal cream bowl. 356. Carved wooden orange cup. 357. Silver-plated flower stands, a cake basket, claret jug, and bottle stand.

Pages 66–67

359. Escritoire of white wood. 360. Albert cottage pianoforte harmonium. 361. Tapestry screen. 362. Wine cooler of light blue porcelain. 363. Chair with tapestry. 364. Ornamental jug. 365. Colored-glass decanter. 366. Cup in the Louis Quatorze style. 367. Beauvais-ware vase. 368. Boxwood saltcellar. 369. Carved wooden cabinet.

Pages 68–69

370. Ivory book cover. 371. Brooch with winged figures. 372. Brooch with rubies and brilliants. 373-377. Enameled breast ornaments with precious stones.

Pages 70–71

378. Stoneware tea urn. 379. Ornamental fringe for a window. 380. Silver vase. 381. Dark rosewood table. 382, 383. Chairs carved from locust tree wood. 384. Embossed porcelain flower vase. 385. Pianoforte that turns into a table. 386. Ornamental bracket. 387. Opalescent vase. 388. Grand piano inlaid with ebony accented with gold relief.

Pages 72–73

389. Stone statue of the virgin and savior. 390. Window of stained and painted glass. 391. Oak screen in the Gothic style. 392. Monumental brass design. 393. Glass vase with silver accents. 394. Table top made of various types of marble. 395. Tripod flower stand. 396. Eight-day clock. 397. Medieval-style fire grate.

Pages 74–75

398. Filigree flower vase of gold threads. 399. Silver-gilt cup in the cinquecento style. 400. Ornamental stoneware vase. 401. Glass wine decanter. 402. Crown imperial plant centerpiece. 403. Silver claret jug. 404, 406. Enameled rings with precious stones. 405. Covered vase. 407. Toilet glass. 408. Papier-mâché ladies cabinet. 409. Jewelry box. 410. Salt cellar. 411. Ivory casket. 412. Gold brooch with carbuncle and brilliants. 413. Damask pattern. 414. Gas lamp and bracket.

Pages 76–77

415. Detail from a damask curtain. 416. Bottom portion of a large frame. 417. Tazza with snakes, foliage, and flowers. 418, 420. Parian jugs. 419. Detail from a paper hanging.

Pages 78–79

421. Louis Quatorze style tureen. 422. Carved ebony table. 423. Mirror with a metal frame. 424. Wooden prayer desk. 425. Sideboard of locust tree wood. 426. Dressing table, chair, and footstool. 427. Wedgwood vases. 428. Coal box of japanned iron. 429. Ebony cabinet with brass gilt molding and ornaments, panels of tortoiseshell, and buhl inlays. 430. Ebony casket with gilt openwork mountings and coral cameos.

Pages 80–81

431. Centerpiece used as an epergne and a candelabrum. 432, 435. Gas chandeliers. 433. Candelabrum of bronze and gilt. 434. Chandelier. 436. Detail from a chatelaine. 437. Candelabrum with Prometheus. 438. Brass chandelier. 439, 440. Silver candelabrums. 441. Brass lamp. 442. Girandole.

Pages 82–83

443. Table knife. 444. Bracket of gutta percha. 445. Cabinet of dark wood with marble and stone inlays. 446. Console table and frame of gutta percha. 447. Fish slice. 448. Magneto-plated silver tray. 449, 450. Porcelain vases. 451. Sideboard. 452. Pinewood frame.

Pages 84–85

453. Detail of a carpet. 454. Knife and sheath. 455. Top of a tazza with silver gilding and chasing. 456. Iron knocker. 457. Embossed

porcelain dessert plate. 458. Terra-cotta font. 459. Caen stone baptismal font. 460. Crusader chess table of ivory.

Pages 86–87
461. Porcelain jelly or cream stand. 462. Embossed ewer. 463. Triangular fruit basket. 464. Silver looking glass. 465. Agricultural vase. 466. Vase of labor. 467. Figure head of a ship. 468. Medieval-style bracelet. 469. Silk design. 470. Vase of oxidized silver. 471. Paper hanging.

Pages 88–89
472, 479. Bronze bell pulls. 473, 480, 481. Brackets. 474. Cupid on a panther. 475. Flower holder. 476. Metal curtain pin. 477. Oak caryatide. 478. Cinquecento-style chimneypiece and bookcase. 482. Small vase. 483. Classical fountain. 484. Ebony tripod. 485. Porcelain lamp.

Pages 90–91
486. Brussels carpet. 487, 489, 490, 494. Details from a chatelaine. 488, 492. Silver brooches. 491. Aiguillette of diamonds, pearls, and an emerald. 493. Tiara of diamonds and sapphires.

Pages 92–93
495. Door knocker. 496. Lamp. 497. Elizabethan looking glass. 498. Rock crystal candlestick with silver and gilt. 499. Candelabrum. 500. Chimneypiece and grate. 501. Brass chandelier. 502. Ornamental flowerpot stand. 503. Carved walnut table. 504. Centerpiece for eight lights.

Pages 94–95
505. Flower basket. 506. Wine cooler. 507. Silver vase for perfume. 508. Silk pattern. 509. Silver gilt tankard. 510. Globe. 511. Fruit basket. 512. Coal vase. 513. Enameled cup. 514. A jeweled, chased, and enameled coffer. 515. Clasp.

Pages 96–97
516-520. Razors. 521. Detail from a carpet. 522. Silver claret jug with enamel. 523. Glass vase. 524. Porcelain vase. 525. Gas chandelier.

Pages 98–99
526. Butter knife. 527, 531. Ornamental spoons. 528, 536. Fish knives. 529, 530. Sugar ladles. 532. Tea caddy spoon. 533. Back and front view of salt spoon. 534. Ivory knife handle. 535. Egg spoon. 536. Fish knives. 537. Dessert spoon.

Pages 100–101
538. Salt cellar. 539. Interior of an iron cup. 540. Ladies' worktable. 541. Decorative table. 542. Tea urn. 543. Coat-of-arms scissors. 544. Vase with silver ornaments. 545. Centerpiece with candles and a glass dish. 546. Salver.

Pages 102–103
547. Chessboard and figures of gold and silver with jewels and enamels. 548. Font. 549. Oak bookcase. 550. Taper stand. 551. Drawer handle. 552. Chandelier. 553. Lectern. 554. Crystal decanter. 555. Carved walnut sideboard.

Pages 104–105
556. Inkstand. 557. Terra-cotta vase. 558. Etagerer, claret jugs, and salt cellars. 559. Fountain. 560. Detail from a carpet.

Pages 106–107
561. Wine cooler. 562. Wedgwood vase. 563. Detail from a table cover. 564. Table. 565. Terra-cotta vase for plants. 566. Papiermâché table. 567. Bronze figure "Ariel directing the Storm." 568. Pedestal. 569. Gothic vase. 570. Window bolt. 571. Jewel case. 572. Screen.

Pages 108–109
573. Cast iron doorknocker. 574. Floor cloth. 575, 577. Crystal jars. 576. Vase. 578, 580. Album covers. 579. Opalescent vase.

Pages 110–111
581. Embroidery trimming. 582. Piano forte of rosewood. 583. Crystal decanter. 584. Terra-cotta vase. 585. Vase. 586, 588. Decorative table. 587. Assiette Montée. 589. Etruscan-style jug. 590. Jewel case and stand. 591. Oak cabinet. 592. Wooden vase.

Pages 112–113
593-599, 601, 603. Brooches. 600. Granite bracelet. 602. Gold ring. 604. Water jug. 605. Table. 606. Vase. 607. Whip handle. 608. Epergne. 609. State bed. 610. Flask.

Pages 114–115
611. Ladies' worktable. 612, 614. Carved chairs. 613. Porcelain vase. 615. Baptismal font. 616. Carved bible cover. 617. Biddur vase. 618. Vine leaf jug.

Pages 116–117
619, 622. Coffee pots. 620, 621, 624. Teapots. 623. Marble chimneypiece. 625, 626. Figures carrying baskets. 627. Top of Couteau de Chasse. 628. Fruit basket. 629. Walnut cabinet.

Pages 118–119
630, 633. Hand bell. 631. Embossed leather chair. 632, 637, 638, 641. Ornamental chairs. 634. Detail from a carpet. 635. Knife handle. 636. Skewer handle. 639. Casket. 640. Walnut sideboard.

Page 120
642, 648. Fowling pieces. 643. Pistol. 644. Highland claymore sword. 645. Gun stock. 646. Officer's field sword. 647. Cavalry dress saber. 649. Scimitar and scabbard.